paper home

paper home

Beautifully unique
origami projects

ESTHER THORPE

Contents

Introduction

It'd be impossible to put a date on it, exactly when my obsession with making things from paper began. Even when I was at preschool I remember endlessly making paper homes for my cuddly toys. My parents were brilliant at encouraging me to be creative, even though creativity wasn't something that came naturally to them.

My mum would frequently take me to exhibitions both locally and further afield, and I distinctly remember being struck by the beautiful work of Bridget Riley on a visit to the Tate Gallery in London. This sparked my fascination with geometric pattern, and with Bridget Riley books, of which I have a library!

At school, art, design and maths were my favourite subjects, and when I went to university to study graphic design, I discovered that origami marries these three passions together beautifully. Throughout my degree and since, I have enjoyed stretching myself with more and more complex models and still find there is nothing more satisfying than transforming 2D square sheets into 3D models.

I live in a small seaside town in the south east of England, with my husband, daughter and two house rabbits, Hugo and Florence (my paper offcuts nibblers!). I enjoy being a mummy by day and a ninja folder by night. I find origami truly addictive and I hope my book will inspire you too. There are projects of varying levels of difficulty: some are straightforward and quick to complete, while others are a little more time consuming, but well worth the effort.

If you are a novice, the Triangular Basket or the Star Garland is a good place to start. Mastering projects that use a similar origami technique is also a good way to develop your folding skills; for example, the Photo Holder, the Cube (Geometric Mobile) and the Vase are all based on the same origami module (the sonobe).

Feel free to dip in and out – the photo step-by-steps should make it easy to pick up where you left off. I also find a good cup of coffee and a little background noise helpful when getting my fold on! Whatever works for you, relax and enjoy your creative process.

Esther

The Importance of Paper

If you're not already obsessed with beautiful papers, once you start folding, there'll be no stopping you! When looking for papers to fold, there are a few practicalities to consider. If you want to make the projects using the exact same papers as I have, see pages 140 and 141.

What will happen to the paper's pattern once it is folded?

Generally speaking, it's best to opt for a small pattern so the design gets celebrated in the finished project rather than lost in the folds.

How many intricate folds are involved in making my chosen project?

Each project will require different paper densities, defined by the 'gsm' (grams per square metre). For lots of delicate folding – the birds on the Crane Mobile, for example – a lighter weight paper (90gsm) is best, but a project requiring the paper to hold its structure – the Lampshade, for instance – will need a heavier paper (120gsm).

Is the paper available in the size I need?

Packs of origami paper are readily available in craft stores in the most frequently used sizes, from standard 15 x 15cm (6 x 6in) squares to smaller 7.5 x 7.5cm (3 x 3in) or larger 25 x 25cm (10 x 10in) sheets.

Can I use paper not specially made for origami?

There are so many beautiful papers available it would be a crime to limit yourself to origami papers only. Other brilliant papers include flat wrap, maps, out-of-date calendars, scrapbook and graph paper.

How do I know what gsm a paper is?

When a gsm is not specified for the paper you want to use – if using recycled papers, for example – you may not be sure of its weight. Compare it to a paper in your collection that you do know the gsm of. And, if you still aren't sure, simply give it a go – you'll soon discover if the paper you have chosen is the right thickness (or not!) for your chosen project.

How can I cut non-standard papers to size?

While scissors can be used to trim paper squares and strips to size, you will find that a guillotine is invaluable for cutting paper accurately; if you have one of these, even if only an A4 sized one, most papers will be adaptable for use.

What other tools do I need?

The answer is, not a lot, but there are a few things that will come in handy: scissors, for cutting ribbon, hook-and-loop tape and double-sided tape; ribbon, for hanging finished projects (3mm wide satin ribbon is most useful as it is narrow enough to be threaded); a large-eyed sewing needle, for threading hanging ribbons; and quick-drying glue, for when origami models need to be secured in place.

How to Fold

Origami, like so many things in life, takes practice to perfect, so take a little time to hone your folding techniques. Always work in a well-lit room. If you're not blessed with daylight, grab a lamp and pop it beside you – folding is so much more enjoyable when you can see what you're doing. Relax and have fun!

ACCURATE FOLDS

It might sound obvious, but making your folds as accurate as possible is fairly crucial. Attention to folding detail will pay off by the end of your model.

Folding in half horizontally and vertically: It is important to ensure the edges of your paper are perfectly aligned before making a fold. Pinch down in the centre and continue the fold out to the edges.

TIP / Don't be afraid to refold – if the precreases aren't in the right place, you may not achieve the results you want, so get it right before it's too late.

Folding in half diagonally: When folding diagonal folds, the paper can occasionally misbehave and slide out of place, so it is crucial to begin by lining up the two opposing corners. Then you can go on to crease in the centre and continue the fold out to the sides.

On this completed sonobe module, the two outer folds are mountain folds and in the centre there is a valley fold.

MOUNTAIN AND VALLEY FOLDS

Throughout the book I refer to 'mountain' and 'valley' folds. The best way to understand this terminology is to think quite simply if the paper is acting as a mountain or a valley. When creating a mountain fold, the model's uppermost side is exposed when folded; when creating a valley fold, the model's uppermost side is enclosed in the fold.

INVERSE FOLDS

One of the trickier folds to master is inverse folding. This is where precreases in the paper are inverted on themselves, as you can see being worked here. This is one half of the Party Diamonds model.

TIP / The best way to check if you've inversed a fold correctly is to ask yourself, are all creases now folded in the opposite direction?

HANG

Party Diamonds

These diamonds are so elegant. They break lots of origami rules with the need for both gluing and cutting but the end result will win over even the most purist of paper folders. They look fabulous hanging on a Christmas tree but can be used all year round. Start by folding them from 15cm (6in) paper squares, and once you've mastered these, experiment with 30cm (12in) scrapbook paper sheets to make the giant versions.

You will need

- 15 x 15cm / 6 x 6in (90gsm) paper / 2 squares
- Scissors
- 3mm (⅛in) ribbon / approx. 30cm (12in)
- Quick-drying glue

Finished size

9cm (3½in) high x 9cm (3½in) diameter

METHOD

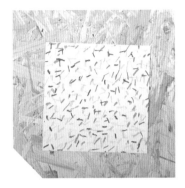

1. Take one paper square, patterned side face up.

2. Fold it in half diagonally.

3. Unfold. Rotate the paper 90 degrees and fold again in the opposite diagonal direction.

4. Unfold and turn the paper over so the white side faces up.

5. Fold in half horizontally.

6. Unfold. Rotate the paper 90 degrees and fold in half horizontally.

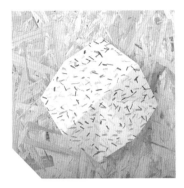

7. Unfold and turn the paper over so the patterned side is face up.

8. Using the precreases, fold the paper into a flat diamond shape, ensuring the two opposing diagonal folds are inverted.

9. With the open edges at the bottom, fold the top right-hand edge to align with the centre fold.

10. Repeat step 9 on the left-hand side.

11. Turn your model over and repeat steps 9 and 10.

12. Remove the triangle at the tip of your model by cutting straight across it using scissors.

13. Unfold the front right-hand fold. Slide your thumb in between the fold to inverse the fold, so that the outside fold is now in the centre.

14. Repeat step 13 three more times around the model – essentially, the paper should be concertinaed in a circle.

15. Rotate the model 180 degrees, so the cut edge is at the top. Fold the top right-hand corner down to align with the centre fold.

16. Repeat step 15 on the top left-hand corner.

17. Repeat steps 15 and 16 around the model (six times more).

18. Unfold the folds created in steps 15–17.

19. Use the precreases to inverse these folds (eight in total).

20. Take the second paper square and repeat steps 1–19 to make the second half of your model.

21. Choose which half you'd like the diamond to be hung from and cut a small slit at the tip of it.

22. Fold the ribbon in half and thread the cut ends through the slit; tie a knot to secure it in place.

23. You have created a hanging loop; gently pull on the loop to position the knot at the tip of the model half. Using quick-drying glue, seal the ribbon in place to complete the hanging loop. Gently spread a thin line of glue onto the inverted triangles at the top edges of this half of your model.

24. Now fix the two halves of your model together: hold one half in each hand and gently rotate to ensure the edges meet neatly.

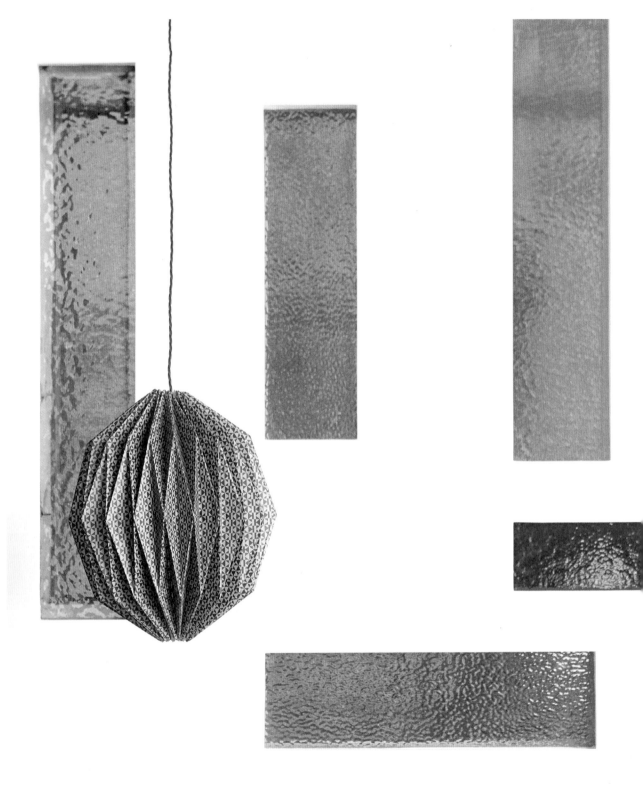

Lampshade

You can create a bespoke interior accessory by folding your own lampshade from the paper of your choice. This origami model uses the art of accordion folding, and it has been developed to hold a traditional lampshade ring. The finished shade encloses perfectly around a ceiling light, and it looks fabulous when made in a geometric patterned paper. The accordion folding starts with lots of preparatory precreasing.

You will need

- 45 x 64cm / 17¾ x 25in paper (120gsm) / 3 sheets
- Quick-drying glue
- Scissors
- White self-adhesive hook-and-loop tape / approx. 60cm (23½in)
- Narrow ribbon or string / 16 pieces each approx. 5cm (2in) long
- Lampshade ring / 25cm (10in) diameter
- LED light bulb

Finished size

35cm (13¾in) high x 30cm (12in) diameter

METHOD

1. Take one sheet of paper, patterned side face up, and fold it in half vertically.

2. Unfold. Fold each side to align with the centre fold, and unfold.

3. Fold the right-hand edge to the first fold on the right-hand side.

4. Now fold the left-hand edge to the first fold on the right-hand side.

5. Unfold. Your paper sheet should now look like this.

6. Repeat steps 3–5 on the left-hand side of the paper, folding first the left-hand edge to the first fold on the left, then the right-hand edge to the same fold. Unfold.

7. Now fold the paper sheet to make precreases halfway between the precreases created in steps 3–6.

8. Once this stage is complete, your paper sheet should look like this.

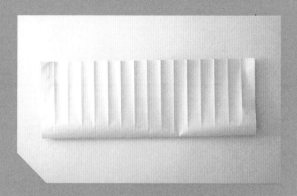

9. Fold the paper in half horizontally and then unfold.

10. Fold the bottom and top edges to the centre fold to create two more horizontal precreases, and unfold.

11. Turn the paper over. Beginning in the bottom left-hand corner, fold diagonally from the horizontal centre fold through two rectangles (from second rectangle up from bottom left through to second rectangle along from bottom left), taking care to ensure the fold sits neatly in the rectangles.

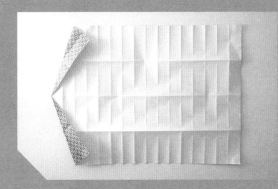

12. Make a mirror image fold to the precrease created in step 11 (from the second rectangle down from the top left through to the second rectangle along from the top left). Unfold both folds.

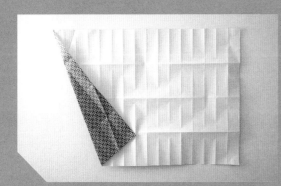
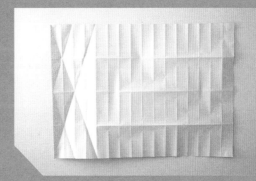

13. Now make a precrease from the top left-hand corner through four rectangles, again ensuring the fold sits neatly in the rectangles, corner to corner. This fold should finish at the fourth rectangle from the bottom left-hand corner. Unfold.

14. Make a mirror image fold to the precrease created in step 13 and unfold. You will see that a pattern is emerging, and that every diagonal fold through a rectangle is in the alternate direction to the rectangle it's next to.

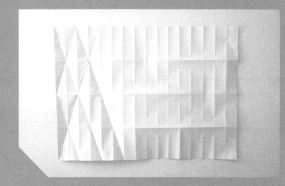

15. Continue with these alternate diagonal precreases until the whole grid is complete and every rectangle has one diagonal fold.

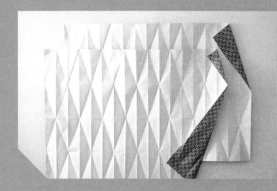

16. Take one of the remaining two paper sheets and repeat steps 1–15. On the last paper sheet, repeat to step 10, then for steps 11–15 make your diagonal precreases in the opposite direction.

17. Take one of the precreased sheets of paper, patterned side face up.

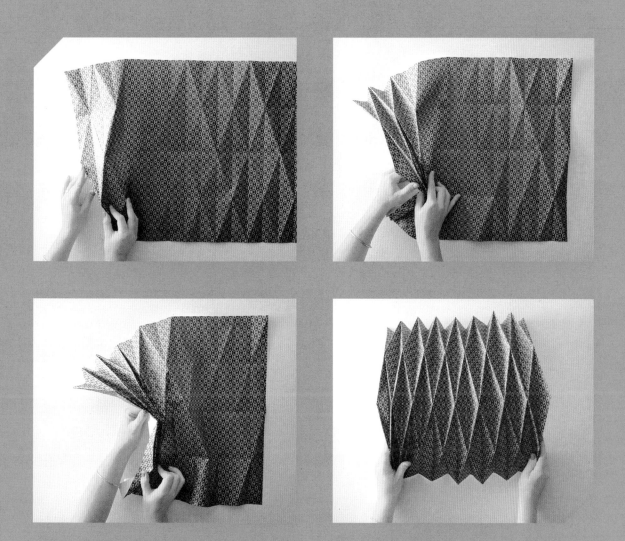

18. Fold the precreases from one end of the paper to the other. This takes a little time to start, but once one end has begun to take shape, the rest of the folds become clearer, with all diagonal folds mountain folds and all vertical folds valley folds. The completed unit is one third of the lampshade. Repeat this step to make two more units from your remaining paper sheets.

19. On each unit, stick the smallest triangular shapes at the top and bottom of the structure together using quick-drying glue (there should be eight sections to glue together at each end).

20. Next, use quick-drying glue to attach the folded units to each other, matching edge to edge as accurately as possible. (Note: the unit with the folds created in opposing diagonals should be sandwiched in the middle of the other two units so that the folds alternate).

21. Cut four lengths of hook-and-loop tape and separate to stick the hook strips on one side and the loop strips on the other, so that they can be joined to each other in step 24.

22. Use quick-drying glue to attach two pieces of ribbon to every other inner section of the lampshade, positioning them as centrally as possible.

23. Use the ribbons to tie the lampshade onto the lampshade ring, and evenly distribute the ribbon ties around the frame.

24. Close the lampshade around the ring and seal with the hook-and-loop tape fastening.

To finish, fix the lampshade ring to the cap and base of the light fitting and fit an LED light bulb.

Christmas Stars

Christmas stars are an excellent way to start experimenting with modular origami. They look brilliant when finished but only require six modules, so have a medium level of difficulty. They are the perfect decoration for the Christmas tree and can be hung around the home all year round. Feel free to experiment with the size of your paper squares – it's tricky to go much smaller than 5cm (2in) square but you can fold the stars as big as you fancy.

You will need

- 15 x 15cm / 6 x 6in paper (90–120gsm) / 6 squares
- 3mm (⅛in) ribbon / approx. 30cm (12in)
- Large-eyed sewing needle

Finished size

15cm (6in) high x 15cm (6in) wide

METHOD

1. Take one paper square, patterned side face up.

2. Fold it in half vertically.

3. Fold the top side in half again, ensuring the open edge sits neatly against the centre fold.

4. Turn the paper over and repeat step 3.

5. Unfold the paper and rotate 90 degrees.

6. Repeat steps 2–5 – this time the folds are being made in the opposite direction.

paper home

7. Unfold the paper.

8. Fold the paper in half diagonally.

9. Unfold the paper, then turn it over and fold it along the opposing diagonal to the fold made in step 8.

10. Unfold the paper so that the patterned side is face up.

11. Using the precreases you've made, fold the two opposing corners with diagonal mountain folds, while also tucking the two opposing corners with valley folds (note: the central square of precreases should be left untouched).

12. Now use the precreases in the central square to create inverse folds, so the module neatly folds into a cross shape.

 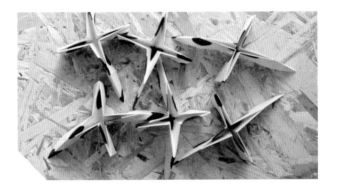

13. You have now completed one module. Repeat steps 1–13 on the remaining paper squares.

14. You have now completed six modules. The modules will now be folded into one another to create the foundation for your star model as shown in steps 15–20.

15. Take two modules: slot a short spoke of one module into a long spoke of the other, ensuring that the small spoke nestles at precisely 90 degrees to the other module.

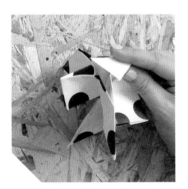  

16. Now take the top triangular section of the longer spoke and inverse the precreases to secure the smaller spoke that has been slotted in.

17. Take a third module and repeat steps 15 and 16 on the opposite small spoke.

18. Turn the model over and repeat this same process with a fourth module, tucking the two short spokes into the two long spokes.

19. Now take a fifth module, find an unfinished side to your model and repeat the process. (This time you will need to insert two short spokes from the existing model, as well as inserting two from the new module.)

20. Turn the model over and repeat step 19 with the final module to complete the foundation model.

21. Using the sewing needle, thread your ribbon through one corner of the foundation model about 1cm from the edge, and tie a knot to create a hanging loop.

22. Now complete the folding to turn the foundation model into the finished star. Gently fold back one folded edge diagonally from the centre to the outer edges, folding it about halfway, to create a point as shown.

23. Repeat step 22 on the adjoining folded edge.

24. Continue to fold each edge in turn, working your way around the model. Take your time over this as it is easy to accidentally rip the paper. Once every edge has been folded down, your Christmas star is complete.

Geometric Mobile

There are so many gorgeous geometric shapes that can be created from paper and I have chosen three of my favourites to be displayed on this super little mobile. The pyramid shape (not quite a pyramid, not quite a septagon!) looks brilliant from all angles, making it perfect for hanging. The cube is made from sonobe modules, and, as with most modular origami, seeing the units come together is a wonder. The elegant octahedron is based on a design by Jeremy Shafer – the success of this shape is all in the precreases, so it's not one to rush.

You will need

- **15 x 15cm and 10 x 10cm / 6 x 6in and 4 x 4in paper (90–120gsm) / 3 squares for each pyramid, 6 squares for each cube and 1 square for each octahedron**
- **Scissors**
- **3mm (⅛in) ribbon / approx. 2m (2yd)**
- **Embroidery hoop**

Finished size

Pyramid: 10 x 9cm & 7 x 6cm (4 x 3½in & 2¾ x 2in)
Cube: 5.5 x 5.5cm & 4 x 4cm (2¼ x 2¼in & 1½ x1½in)
Octahedron: 10 x 6cm & 6 x 4cm (4 x 2 & 2 x 1½in)

METHOD: PYRAMID

1. Take one paper square, white side face up, and fold it in half diagonally.

2. Fold the bottom right-hand corner to the top corner.

3. Fold the bottom left-hand corner to the top corner.

4. Unfold the left- and right-hand folds, and then fold the triangle in half.

5. Repeat steps 1–4 on the remaining paper squares to give you three modules.

6. Take two of your modules and insert one into the other as shown (note: the two open ends of one module slot into the folded end of the other).

7. Repeat step 6 to slot the remaining module into your model.

8. Complete the pyramid by connecting the open ends together in the same way (note: as you insert one into the other, refolding the precreases will help).

9. Cut a 20cm length of ribbon and tie a knot close to one end. Slightly loosen one join in the pyramid and insert the knot in between the modules.

10. Realign the modules to secure the ribbon in place. Repeat steps 1–10 to make a second pyramid for your mobile. To make pyramids in different sizes, vary the size of the paper squares.

METHOD: CUBE

1. Take one paper square, white side face up, and fold it in half horizontally.

2. Unfold. Fold the right-hand edge to align with the centre fold.

3. Fold the left-hand edge to align with the centre fold.

4. Open the fold on the right-hand side and fold the top corner diagonally to align with the opened fold. Then refold back to the centre.

5. Rotate the model 180 degrees and repeat step 4.

6. Make a diagonal fold from the bottom right-hand corner, running in line with the diagonal fold made in step 5.

7. Tuck the diagonal fold made in step 6 underneath the left-hand fold.

8. Rotate the model 180 degrees and repeat steps 6 and 7.

9. Turn the model over. Fold the bottom left-hand corner up to meet the top left-hand corner, creating a right angle.

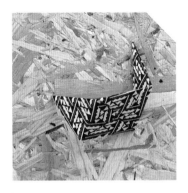

10. Fold the top right-hand corner down to meet the bottom right-hand corner, creating a square. This completes one sonobe module.

11. Repeat steps 1–10 on the remaining paper squares to give you six sonobe modules.

12. Take two of the modules and insert the triangular end on one into a slot at the central square of the other, ensuring that the right angles are lined up.

13. Take a third module and insert it into one of the attached modules in the same way.

14. Continue to add modules to form the six sides of the cube, stopping before you secure the final module in place to add a 20cm length of ribbon for hanging as described in step 15.

15. Tie a knot close to one end of the ribbon; insert it into the model before slotting in the final point.

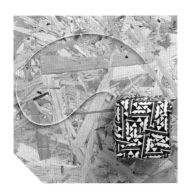

16. The finished cube. Repeat steps 1–15 to make a second cube for your mobile.

METHOD: OCTAHEDRON

1. Take one paper square, white side face up, and fold it in half horizontally.

2. Unfold. Fold up the bottom edge to align with the centre fold.

3. Fold down the top edge to align with the centre fold.

4. Unfold the paper square. Rotate 90 degrees and fold in half horizontally.

5. Take the bottom right-hand corner and fold it diagonally from the centre fold to the furthest fold on the right-hand side.

6. Repeat step 5 on the left-hand side.

7. Unfold the right-hand side. Inverse fold the precrease created in step 5.

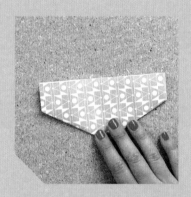

8. Unfold the left-hand side and repeat step 7 to inverse fold the precrease created in step 6.

9. Fold the top layer of the right-hand side to the centre fold, as shown. Then repeat on the left-hand side of the model.

10. Turn the model over and fold each side to the centre fold.

 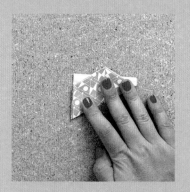 

11. Create mountain folds following the diagonals that can be seen across the model: from the top right corner to just above the bottom left corner, and from the top left corner to just above the bottom right corner. Turn the model over and repeat these folds on the opposite side.

 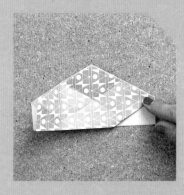 

12. Unfold the folds created in steps 9 and 10. Create a diagonal fold on the top layer of the bottom right-hand corner using the precreases you have made. This fold needs to be tucked into the model to make a mountain fold.

13. Repeat to fold each of the remaining corners of the model as described in step 12.

14. Take the triangular section on the right-hand side and inverse fold the precreases as shown. Turn the model over and repeat.

15. Pick up the model and pinch in both the right- and left-hand sides as well as the front and back; this will allow the model to begin to take its shape from the precreases you have made.

16. Once the octahedron has formed, you'll see there are four excess triangular shapes. Fold the triangles in pairs to align with the 3D shape.

geometric mobile

17. In each pair, there will be one triangle that's smaller than the other. Working on one of the pairs and using the larger triangle as a pocket, fold the smaller triangle into it. Cut a 20cm length of ribbon and tie a knot close to one end.

18. Insert the knot into the model before joining the final pair of triangles to complete the shape.

19. Repeat steps 1–18 to make a second octahedron for your mobile.

The shapes can be made from different sized paper squares to add variety to your mobile.

METHOD: MOBILE ASSEMBLY

1. Take the embroidery hoop and arrange your shapes around it. Secure the shapes in place by wrapping their ribbons around the inner hoop.

2. Cut two lengths of ribbon for hanging the mobile, and secure it in place by wrapping each end of the ribbon around the inner hoop on opposite sides (see page 42).

SHELF

Daisy

This six-petal flower is traditionally made using three
US dollars, which explains why it is also known as an origami
dollar flower! Daisies are a great addition to a paper bouquet
and they are the simplest to fold of the three flowers I have
included in this book. Due to its simple shape this flower
lends itself well to being folded from patterned papers, so try
experimenting to add a whole new look to your bouquet.

You will need

- 6.5 x 15cm / 2½ x 6in paper (90gsm) / 3 rectangles
- 3mm (⅛in) ribbon / approx. 10cm (4in) / 3 lengths
- Bamboo skewer
- Quick-drying glue
- Scissors

Finished size

5cm (2in) high x 5cm (2in) wide

METHOD

1. Take one paper rectangle, white side face up, and place it in a landscape direction. Fold it in half vertically.

2. Unfold. Fold the right-hand edge a third of the way towards the centre fold.

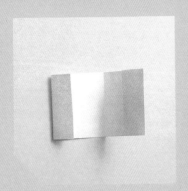

3. Fold the left-hand edge a third of the way towards the centre fold.

4. Fold in half horizontally, and then unfold.

5. Fold the bottom right-hand corner diagonally towards the centre fold.

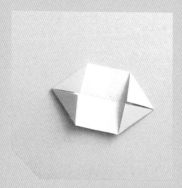

6. Repeat step 5 on the remaining three corners.

7. Fold the bottom edge to the centre fold.

8. Fold the top edge to the centre fold.

9. Make a valley fold through the centre.

10. Keeping the edges of the model together, make another valley fold, this time vertically through the centre to create a V-shaped unit.

11. Repeat steps 1–10 on the remaining rectangles of paper to give you three V-shaped units.

12. Take two of the V-shaped units and pinch them together at their centre points.

13. Using the ribbon, tie the units tightly together at the centre.

14. Attach the remaining V-shaped unit in the same way, making sure it is tied to both units.

15. Trim the excess ribbon, allowing sufficient length to tie the flower to the 'stalk' (see step 16). Holding the flower with the ribbons underneath, carefully shape each petal.

paper home

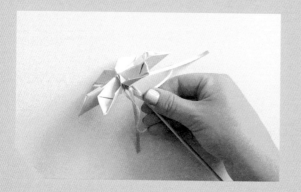

16. Take your bamboo skewer and position the flower at one end. Neatly wrap the ribbon ends around the stalk. Secure the ribbon in place with quick-drying glue.

daisy

Rose

Origami roses are a wonderful way to add excitement to a bouquet of paper flowers, although a single rose displayed in a vase has quite an impact too. They are slightly more challenging to make than the six-petal daisy (page 58) or the elegant lily (page 74) but you will find the process incredibly satisfying. Don't feel disheartened if it takes a few attempts to perfect – it'll be so worth it.

You will need

- **20 x 20cm / 8 x 8in paper (90gsm) / 1 square**
- **Bamboo skewer**
- **Quick-drying glue**

Finished size

Approx. 4cm (1½in) diameter

METHOD

1. Begin with the paper square white side face up and fold it in half horizontally.

2. Unfold. Rotate 90 degrees and fold in half horizontally again.

3. Unfold. Fold one edge to align with the centre fold, and then fold the opposite edge to meet it.

4. Unfold your paper sheet and repeat step 3 in the opposite direction.

5. Unfold. Now fold the bottom edge up to the top precrease.

6. Unfold. Rotate the paper to repeat step 5 at each side of the square.

7. Precreases are now needed in between the folds made in steps 5 and 6. Carefully fold and unfold to create these, using the centre fold and previous folds as a guide.

8. You should now have a grid of lots of precreases as shown.

9. Turn the paper over and fold each corner diagonally to the first precrease from the outer edge.

10. Fold the paper in half diagonally.

11. Unfold. Rotate 90 degrees and fold in half diagonally again. Unfold.

12. Refold the model diagonally. Now partly unfold this fold, but as you do so create a new fold. This fold will dissect the white triangle at the side edge and will end near the centre of the model, at the corner of the precreases created in step 7. Unfold.

13. Rotate the paper and repeat step 12 on each side of the square. When you have completed this step, the diagonal precreases you have just made should look like a pinwheel.

14. While holding the paper in the centre, carefully refold all the diagonal precreases at the same time to create a small circle – it will almost spiral in on itself.

15. At one corner, lift the horizontal and vertical precreases to form a box-like shape. These folds should fall into place easily, but will need some refolding to confirm the structure.

16. Repeat step 15 at each corner.

17. Taking the bottom left-hand corner of one box shape, fold the corner diagonally. Unfold.

18. Using this precrease, fold the diagonal towards the top tip of the white triangle.

19. Repeat steps 17 and 18 at each corner.

20. Now take one flat edge and fold it diagonally towards the next box fold.

21. Repeat step 20 three more times around the model.

22. Taking a box edge, flatten it towards its neighbouring fold (created in steps 20 and 21). Fold the two small triangles at the bottom in on themselves. As you create these folds, you will find that the model will spiral around on itself; allow it to do so as much as possible, as this will help the construction of the rose.

23. Repeat step 22 at each box edge, then tuck all the white corners underneath the model to create a square base.

24. Turn the model over to reveal your rose. The rose petals will be fairly tightly packed together, so carefully shape them to your preference.

25. Turn the rose over and attach a bamboo skewer 'stalk' to the centre of the base of the rose, using quick-drying glue.

paper home

Lily

Lilies are a classic origami flower that are an intricate and impressive fold. They add a unique dimension to a bouquet and sit really well alongside other flowers. Practice makes perfect with these blooms but they are more fiddly than complicated to make. For this reason it's really important to use a thin, plain paper, or one with minimal pattern.

You will need

- **15 x 15cm / 6 x 6in paper (90gsm) / 1 square**
- **Bamboo skewer**
- **Quick-drying glue (optional)**

Finished size

5cm (2in) high x 3cm (1¼in) wide

METHOD

1. Begin with the paper square colour side face up. Fold it in half diagonally.

2. Unfold. Rotate 90 degrees and fold in half diagonally again.

3. Unfold.

4. Turn the paper over and fold in half horizontally.

5. Unfold. Rotate 90 degrees and fold in half horizontally again.

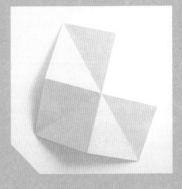

6. Unfold.

7. Using these precreases, fold the paper into a flat diamond shape, ensuring the two opposing diagonal folds are inverted.

8. With the folded edges at the base of the model, fold the top layer of the bottom right-hand edge to align with the centre fold.

9. Repeat step 8 on the left-hand side.

10. Turn the model over and repeat steps 8 and 9 to fold each edge to the centre fold.

11. Unfold one of the side folds. Inverse the fold, so the outer fold is now positioned in the centre of the model.

12. Repeat step 11 on each of the side folds (a total of four inverse folds).

13. Taking one layer from the right-hand side, fold it back to reveal some of the white side of the paper.

14. Fold the top two outer edges to align with the centre of the model and then unfold.

15. Carefully pull the top outer edges of the paper down, using the precreases to create a small diamond shape.

lily

16. Fold the lower edge of the diamond shape up to create a small triangle.

17. Fold the top layer over as shown, and repeat steps 14–16 until the whole model is at this stage.

18. Fold over the top layer to reveal a diamond with no edges exposed.

19. Fold the lower outer edges of the top layer to align with the centre fold.

20. Repeat steps 18 and 19 until the whole model is at this stage.

21. Take one of the long triangles at the top of the model and gently pull it down. Use your thumb and index finger to gently manipulate the paper into a petal. Repeat to curve the remaining three petals into shape.

22. You now have your finished lily.

23. Take your bamboo skewer and gently pierce it through the centre of the lily to make the stalk. When you are happy with its position, you might wish to secure the skewer in place with a drop of quick-drying glue, but the paper will usually hold it sufficiently.

Vase

This origami vase provides a beautiful geometric base for your blooms. The distinctive structure of interlinked pyramid shapes has been made from sonobe modules – a classic unit for modular origami – to create a textured paper panel that sits neatly around a glass jar or cup, which can be filled with water to keep your flowers fresh. It looks brilliant made from a combination of plain and patterned papers.

You will need

- 5 x 5cm / 2 x 2in paper (90 gsm) / approx. 30–40 squares depending on your preferred vase size
- Measuring tape
- Glass jar or cup
- Washi tape or masking tape

Finished size

Approx. 10cm (4in) high x 12.5cm (5in) circumference

METHOD

1. Begin by measuring the dimensions of your jar or cup. Make a note of its height and its circumference at the widest part, and then set it aside.

2. Take one paper square, white side face up, and fold it in half horizontally.

3. Unfold. Fold the right-hand edge to align with the centre fold.

4. Fold the left-hand edge to align with the centre fold.

5. Open the fold on the right-hand side and fold the top corner diagonally to align with the opened fold, as shown. Then refold back to the centre.

paper home

6. Rotate the model 180 degrees and repeat step 5.

7. Make a diagonal fold from the bottom right-hand corner, running in line with the diagonal fold made in step 6.

8. Tuck this fold underneath the left-hand fold.

9. Rotate 180 degrees and repeat steps 7 and 8.

10. Make a valley fold through the centre.

11. Make a mountain fold by bringing the bottom right-hand point up to the top left-hand corner.

12. Turn the model over, and repeat step 11 to complete your first sonobe module.

13. Repeat steps 2–12 on the remaining paper squares to give you the number of sonobe modules you require. The modules will now be connected together in small pyramid-like shapes, and these will all interconnect together.

14. First, we begin with just three modules. Take two of the modules and insert the 'spike' on one into an opening at the centre of the other, taking care to ensure that the triangles are lined up.

15 Take a third module and insert it into one of the attached modules.

16. Now insert a third spike to complete the pyramid shape.

17. You will now continue to add to this pyramid shape to create a panel of multiple pyramids. Create your next pyramid from one of the spikes coming out of the existing pyramid.

18. Continue to add more of your modules.

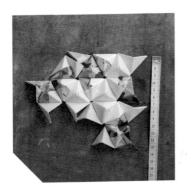 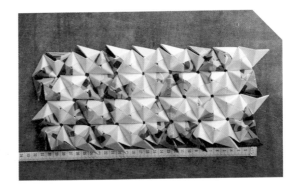

19. Measure as you go to ensure that the height of the panel is slightly taller than your jar or cup and that the width is slightly longer than its circumference. Make sure the modules finish evenly to form a rectangular panel.

20. When the panel is the required dimensions, turn it over and tape along the top and bottom row of excess spikes to neaten.

21. Now lift the panel up and, with the pyramids facing outwards, start to wrap it around to make the vase shape.

22. Join the ends to one another by creating new pyramids where the edges of the panel meet.

23. Finally, carefully place your jar or cup into the centre of your origami structure.

vase

Triangular Basket

These triangular baskets are so aesthetically pleasing, and useful at the same time. Dot them all around your home to store any little bits and bobs. They work particularly well when made with three different papers, but do try to use different tones of the same colour to create a chic look. They are surprisingly easy to make too. Experiment with the paper's gsm to produce a sturdier basket.

You will need

- 15 x 15cm / 6 x 6in paper (120gsm) / 3 squares
- Quick-drying glue

Finished size

4cm (1½in) high x 12cm (4¾in) wide

METHOD

1. Take one paper square, white side face up, and fold it in half diagonally.

2. Fold the bottom right-hand corner to the top corner.

3. Fold the bottom left-hand corner to the top corner.

4. Unfold the left- and right-hand folds. Fold the top corner of the triangle down to align with the precreases made in steps 2 and 3.

5. Repeat steps 1–4 on the remaining paper squares to give you three modules.

6. Take two of your modules and carefully slot one into the other, sandwiching it in between the layers.

7. Ensure the triangles are lined up and refold the precreases to help the join to hold.

triangular basket

8. Repeat steps 6 and 7 to join the third module (note: the middle module is sandwiched in between the layers of the module at either end).

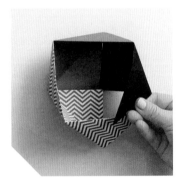

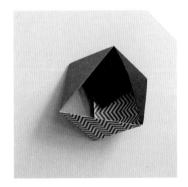

9. Now bring the ends together and slot them into each other as in steps 6 and 7. Add a drop of quick-drying glue between each base layer to make the basket more sturdy.

Photo Holder

Create an origami photo holder using a classic sonobe multi-modular structure as a beautiful base. This geometric shape makes a fantastic accessory for the home and works beautifully with patterned paper. Try experimenting with the size of your paper squares – you could create a small, delicate base by using 8 x 8cm paper, or for a colossal base, use 20 x 20cm sheets.

You will need

- **15 x 15cm / 6 x 6in paper (120gsm) / 12 squares**
- **Clip photo holder**
- **Quick-drying glue**

Finished size

12.5cm (5in) high x 12.5cm (5in) wide

METHOD

1. Take one paper square, white side face up, and fold it in half horizontally.

2. Unfold. Fold the right-hand edge to align with the centre fold.

3. Fold the left-hand edge to align with the centre fold.

4. Open the fold on the right-hand side and fold the top corner diagonally to align with the opened fold. Refold back to the centre.

5. Rotate the model 180 degrees and repeat step 4.

6. Make a diagonal fold from the bottom right-hand corner, running in line with the diagonal fold made in step 5.

7. Open up the left-hand side and tuck the fold created in step 6 underneath the left-hand fold.

8. Rotate the model 180 degrees and repeat steps 6 and 7.

9. Make a valley fold through the centre.

10. Create a mountain fold by bringing the top left-hand corner to the bottom right-hand corner.

11. Turn the model over and repeat step 10 to complete one sonobe module.

12. Repeat steps 1–11 on the remaining paper squares to give you 12 sonobe modules.

13. Take two of the modules and insert the 'spike' on one into an opening at the centre of the other, taking care to ensure that the triangles are lined up.

14. Take a third module and insert it into one of the attached modules as pictured above. Then insert a third spike, to complete a pyramid-like shape.

15. Repeat steps 13 and 14 with the remaining modules to make four pyramid 'clusters' in all.

16. Take two of the clusters and insert one spike into a pocket that's close to an existing pyramid shape.

17. Take the spike to the top left and insert it into the pocket on the top right.

18. Repeat steps 16 and 17 to join the remaining two pyramid clusters.

19. Hold the two halves together – they should fit together like jigsaw pieces. Four more pyramids need to be created to join the halves together: insert spikes into pockets as before, but before forming the final pyramid …

20. … insert your clip photo holder.

21. Complete the folding of the final pyramid and secure the clip photo holder in place with a drop of quick-drying glue.

The round shape of the photo holder is created by slotting together sonobe modules into pyramid-shaped units that are then joined into a ball.

Feltigami Box

I distinctly remember first learning to make these boxes at Brownies when I was just a little girl. Those early models were made from discarded Christmas cards, but I have updated this children's craft project by using fabulous large-scale felt sheets to create a contemporary storage solution that would fit effortlessly into any modern home. The felt is available in a range of colours, but I have chosen a sophisticated grey.

You will need

- 45 x 45cm / 17¾ x 17¾in paper (120gsm) / 1 square
- 42 x 42cm / 16½ x 16½in paper (120gsm) / 1 square
- Scissors
- 60cm-wide (23½in-wide) self-adhesive felt / 1m (1yd) in a colour of your choosing

Finished size

10cm (4in) high x 22.5cm (9in) wide

METHOD

1. Start by making the box lid. Take the large paper sheet (45 x 45cm) and cut a square of felt approx. 2cm bigger all round.

2. Gradually peel back the paper backing from the felt and ease it onto your paper square as neatly as you can.

3. Trim the excess felt around the paper square so that it matches the paper dimensions exactly.

4. With the paper side face up, loosely fold the square in half horizontally: simply pinch the crease at either side; do not fold the entire line.

5. Unfold. Rotate the square 90 degrees and repeat step 4 in the opposite direction. Unfold.

6. Fold from the bottom right-hand corner to the centre, using the crease marks made in steps 4 and 5 to measure how far to fold. The triangle created should have two corners meeting the precreases. Repeat to fold the remaining corners so they all meet in the middle, as shown above, and then unfold.

7. Fold the bottom right-hand corner to the furthest fold. Do ensure all precreases are in line with each other as this will create a much neater finish.

8. Repeat step 7 at each of the three remaining corners.

9. Now fold each corner to its closest fold.

10. Take the bottom right-hand corner back to the centre, refolding the precrease. Lift the felt edge up to a 90-degree angle to create a 'wall' – the precreases you have made should allow this to happen with ease.

11. Rotate your model 180 degrees and repeat step 10 to form another wall at the opposite corner.

12. Rotate the model 90 degrees. Bring the two newly created walls of the box together (where the felt is first folded over). Turn the model onto its side to create triangular folds (as shown top right) and bring the bottom corner up, using the precreases to fold it over to create another wall (as shown bottom left). Tuck the triangle down onto the base of the box.

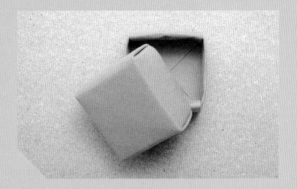

13. Rotate the model 180 degrees and repeat step 12 at the remaining corner to complete the box lid.

14. To make the box base, take the remaining (smaller) sheet of paper and repeat steps 1–13.

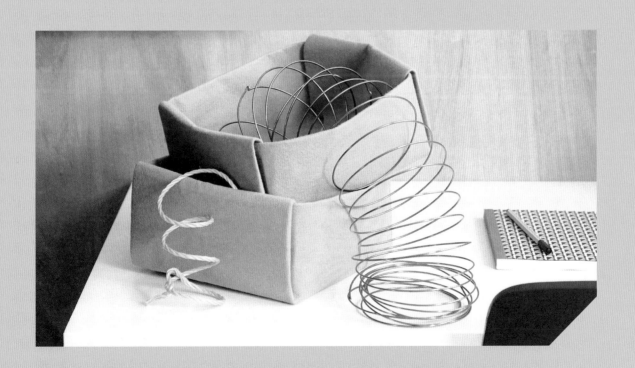

WALL

Star Garland

This pretty little garland looks great made from simple white paper – the perfect decoration for a wedding party perhaps? But I couldn't resist giving mine a punch of colour, alternating stars made from a neutral grey patterned paper with those created from a bold, bright, neon yellow. You can have endless fun choosing colour schemes, and the more stars you make, the longer your garland will be!

You will need

- 1.5 (½in) x 20cm (8in) paper (90gsm) / 12–20 strips depending on your preferred garland length
- Skewer
- Large-eyed sewing needle
- 3mm (⅛in) ribbon / 1–2m (1–2yd) depending on your preferred garland length
- Scissors
- Quick-drying glue (optional)

Finished size

Each star: approx 2cm (1in) high x 1cm (½in) deep

METHOD

1. Take one of your paper strips and make a loop at one end with the coloured (or patterned) side on the outside of the loop.

2. Feed the shorter end of the paper strip through the loop to create a knot close to the end of the strip.

3. Flatten the fold.

4. Rotate the knot 180 degrees, fold the short end over and tuck it neatly into the knot.

  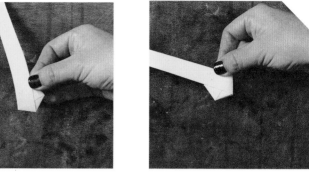

5. Turn the paper strip over and fold the long end over the knot, ensuring the fold is level to the knot's edge.

6. Repeat step 5, and continue to turn and fold the paper strip over the knot to create a small pentagonal shape.

 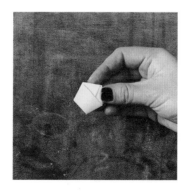 

7. When you reach the end of the paper strip, tuck it into the folded layers of the knot to complete the folded pentagonal shape.

star garland

8. Now to turn the pentagon into a lucky star. Take one corner and pinch together its neighbouring edges between your finger and thumb. Repeat at each corner of the pentagon, and as you do so the shape will slightly inflate to create a star shape.

9. Repeat steps 1–8 for each of your paper strips to make as many stars as you desire.

paper home

10. Use the skewer to pierce a hole through the centre of each star in preparation, then use the large-eyed sewing needle to thread the stars onto your ribbon.

11. Once all the stars are threaded onto the ribbon, distribute them evenly, then cut the ribbon to the desired length.

The threaded stars should sit securely on the ribbon, but add a drop of glue alongside each hole if you wish.

star garland

Crane Mobile

The paper crane is one of the most iconic of all origami models. There is an ancient Japanese legend that says folding 1,000 cranes brings you one wish. That's some task, but you only need to fold a few to make this contemporary hanging. Try experimenting with different papers, and don't be afraid to fold more birds than you need, so you can be picky when it comes to assembling the mobile.

You will need

- **Paper squares varying in size between 10 x 10cm and 20 x 20cm / 4 x 4in and 8 x 8in (90gsm) / 5–10 squares**
- **Large-eyed sewing needle**
- **3mm (⅛in) ribbon / approx. 1m (1yd) to attach cranes to mobile**
- **Scissors**
- **Circular frame / approx. 30cm (12in) diameter (I used a lampshade ring)**
- **Quick-drying glue**
- **5mm ribbon / approx. 1–2m (1–2yd) to hang mobile**

Finished size

Mobile: 30cm (12in) diameter
Paper cranes: vary in size

METHOD

1. Take one paper square, patterned side face up.

2. Fold the paper square in half diagonally.

3. Unfold. Rotate the paper 90 degrees and fold in half diagonally again.

4. Unfold and turn the paper over.

5. Fold in half horizontally.

6. Unfold. Now fold in half vertically.

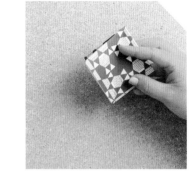

7. Unfold and turn the paper over so the patterned side is face up.

8. Using the precreases, fold the paper into a flat diamond shape, ensuring the two opposing diagonal folds are inverted.

9. With the open edges at the bottom, fold the bottom right-hand edge to align with the centre fold.

10. Now fold the bottom left-hand edge to align with the centre fold.

11. Turn the model over and repeat steps 9 and 10.

12. Fold down the triangle at the top. There is quite a lot of paper to fold, so this might be tough, but persevere as this precrease is essential.

13. Unfold the top triangle, and the left- and right-hand folds.

14. Begin lifting up the top layer of paper while holding the top triangle in place.

15. Continue lifting up the top layer, so the bottom point is now stretched up above the model, while using the precreases to create a long diamond shape.

16. Turn the model over and repeat steps 12–15.

17. Place the model so that the split end of the diamond is at the base. Fold the top layer of the bottom right-hand edge to align with the centre fold.

18. Then fold the top layer of the bottom left-hand edge to align with the centre fold.

19. Turn the model over and repeat steps 17 and 18.

20. Take the bottom left- and right-hand sides as high as possible and create diagonal folds at about 45 degrees to the top of the model (for the head and tail).

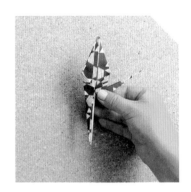

21. Unfold the folds created in step 20. Working first on the bottom right-hand point, inverse the folds. Place your forefinger in the groove between the folds and use your thumb underneath to push the point up inside itself, and press it flat between your finger and your thumb.

22. Repeat step 21 to inverse the folds on the bottom left-hand point.

23. Choose which end you'd like to be the head of the crane and fold down the tip by about a centimetre to create the head shape.

24. Working with an overhead view of your model, gently pull each wing out, which will in turn expand the crane's body.

25. Continue until you are happy with the shape of your crane.

26. Use a large-eyed sewing needle to thread a length of 3mm ribbon through the crane's body; secure with a small knot.

27. Repeat steps 1–26 to make the number of cranes you require for your mobile.

28. Arrange the cranes in the frame and tie a knot in each hanging ribbon before trimming; seal the knots with glue.

29. Cut a length of 5mm ribbon for hanging the mobile. Secure it to the midpoint at the top of the frame and, once again, seal the knot with quick-drying glue.

Pyramid Fairy Lights

I wanted to create a unique origami design that would fully enclose each tiny bulb on a string of fairy lights. The result is these sweet little pyramids that look fabulous, especially when made from a delicately patterned paper. The pyramids are based on the classic origami water-bomb, which you may well already be familiar with, and if not, don't worry – they're beautifully straightforward to fold.

You will need

- 15 x 15cm / 6 x 6in paper (90gsm) / 10 squares
- 5mm (¼in) double-sided tape
- Scissors
- LED fairy lights / 10 bulbs
  (or more if you fancy a challenge)
- Quick-drying glue

Finished size

Each pyramid: approx. 5cm (2in) high x 2.5cm (1in) wide

METHOD

1. Take one paper square, white side face up, and fold it in half diagonally.

2. Unfold. Rotate the paper 90 degrees and fold in half diagonally again.

3. Unfold. Turn the paper over (patterned side face up). Fold in half horizontally in both directions and unfold.

4. Using the precreases, fold the paper into a flat triangle shape, ensuring the two opposing horizontal folds are inverted. Orientate the model so that the open edges are at the bottom.

5. Fold the bottom right-hand edge to align with the centre fold, as shown. Repeat on the left-hand side.

6. Turn the model over and repeat step 5 to fold both sides to the centre fold.

7. Fold the bottom right-hand edge to the centre fold to create a long, triangular shape, as shown. Repeat on the left-hand side.

8. Turn the model over and repeat step 7 to fold both sides to the centre fold.

9. Take the top layer of the right-hand section and fold it down to create a triangle, as shown. Unfold.

10. Open the folds on the right-hand side twice to bring the small triangle fold made in step 9 to the back of the model, and fold this triangle to the front.

11. Refold the right-hand side to the centre to sandwich the small triangle in between the folds.

12. Repeat steps 9–11 on the left-hand side.

13. Turn the model over and repeat steps 9–12.

14. Unfold the folds on the left- and right-hand sides of the model once. Cut a narrow strip of double-sided tape and attach it in between and slightly overlapping the triangles – it should be just long enough to secure them in place; peel off the backing and refold. Turn the model over and repeat.

15. Use scissors to cut approx. 3mm from the end of the model to create a small hole, as shown.

16. Pick up the model so that the hole is facing you, and gently blow into the hole so that the sides of the model expand to make the pyramid shape.

17. Give the pyramid shape clarity by gently reinforcing the edges with your fingers.

18. Repeat steps 1–17 to make more pyramids from your remaining paper squares (I made a total of 10).

19. Take your string of fairy lights and, working on one pyramid at a time, carefully insert a fairy light bulb inside the hole created in step 15.

20. Once all the pyramids have been fitted onto the fairy light bulbs, use quick-drying glue to secure them in place.

Wall Art

Origami is a great way to add texture to your wall display. This small origami 'painting' is beautifully simple to make but provides an impressive piece of homemade art. It is made by combining sonobe modules to create a geometric design. The number of paper squares you use will depend on how big you'd like your picture to be – my picture is a modest 30cm (12in) square but you can fill the entire wall if you choose too!

You will need

- 5 x 5cm / 2 x 2in paper (90gsm) / approx. 18–25 squares
- 30 x 30cm / 12 x 12in scrapbook card
- Quick-drying glue
- 30 x 30cm / 12 x 12in picture frame

Finished size

30cm (12in) high x 30cm (12in) wide

METHOD

1. Take one paper square, white side face up, and fold it in half horizontally.

2. Unfold. Fold the right-hand edge to align with the centre fold.

3. Fold the left-hand edge to align with the centre fold.

4. Turn the model over and fold in half horizontally.

5. Fold the top layer of the model in half diagonally.

6. Unfold and make a diagonal fold in the opposite direction.

7. Turn the model over and repeat steps 5 and 6. Then unfold the diagonal folds, as shown.

8. Open the left-hand side. Fold the bottom left diagonal along its precrease and then fold the left-hand side to the centre again.

9. Open the right-hand side. Fold the top right diagonal along its precrease and then fold the right-hand side to the centre again.

10. Turn the model over and inverse fold the triangular section at one end. Tuck this underneath the fold made in steps 8 and 9 to create an inverted triangular prism.

11. Repeat step 10 at the opposite end of the model, and then turn the model over.

12. Repeat steps 1–11 on your remaining squares of paper.

13. Place the completed shapes onto your piece of scrapbook card and begin to arrange them into a picture.

14. Three shapes fit well together to create hexagons and this is a good starting point.

15. When you are happy with the arrangement, use quick-drying glue to secure the shapes in place.

To finish, place the scrapbook card in the frame.

Project Papers

Where I have used particular papers for my origami models as demonstrated in the step photos, details are provided below. Please see Suppliers for how to contact the manufacturers.

PARTY DIAMONDS (PAGE 14)
Patterned: The Printed Peanut / Spangle

LAMPSHADE (PAGE 22)
Esme Winter / PEGGY in mauve/black

CHRISTMAS STARS (PAGE 33)
Caroline Gardner / BLACK DOT

GEOMETRIC MOBILE (PAGE 42)
Pyramid: Esme Winter / WALTZ in red orange
Cube: Esme Winter / JAZZ in black
Octahedron: Esme Winter / FREQUENCY in light blue

VASE (PAGE 82)
Patterned: Hanna Konola / BLOCKS (note: squares were cut to size from wrap)

TRIANGULAR BASKET (PAGE 90)
Patterned: Mulk / GEOMETRIC double-sided paper (note: squares were cut to size from wrap)

PHOTO HOLDER (PAGE 96)
Esme Winter / STORMONT in charcoal blue

FELTIGAMI BOX (PAGE 104)
Minerva Crafts / Sticky-back self-adhesive acrylic felt fabric

STAR GARLAND (PAGE 114)
Plain: Neon London / NEON YELLOW (note: strips were cut to size from gift wrap)
Patterned: Mulk / GEOMETRIC double-sided paper (note: strips were cut to size from wrap)

CRANE MOBILE (PAGE 120)
Patterned: Esme Winter / KALEIDOSCOPE in navy
Plain: Neon London / NEON RED (note: squares were cut to size from wrap)

PYRAMID FAIRY LIGHTS (PAGE 128)
Esme Winter / STORMONT in peach orange

WALL ART (PAGE 134)
Patterned: Hanna Konola / SNOWSTORM (note: squares were cut to size from wrap)

Suppliers

ESME WINTER
www.esmewinter.co.uk
enquiries@esmewinter.co.uk

THE PRINTED PEANUT
www.theprintedpeanut.co.uk
Also available from:
www.louiselockhart.co.uk

MULK
www.mulk.co.uk
enquiries@mulk.co.uk

NEON LONDON
www.etsy.com/uk/shop/NEONLDN

HANNA KONOLA
www.hannakonola.com
www.wrapmagazine.com
hanna@hannakonola.com

MINERVA CRAFTS
www.minervacrafts.com
+44 (0)1254 708068

CAROLINE GARDNER
www.carolinegardner.com
info@carolinegardner.com

About the Author

Esther Thorpe is an avid origami fan who specialises in multi-modular origami creations. She enjoys celebrating the traditional Japanese art of paper folding while adding a contemporary edge. With a background in both graphic design and teaching primary aged children, Esther also enjoys providing origami workshops. She sells handmade and bespoke origami masterpieces from her website www.origamiest.co.uk.

Acknowledgements

I have such a huge amount of gratitude to those who have been generous with their time, resources, love and support during the creation of this book!

To Amy, Zoe and Cheryl, for the time and expertise they have invested, and to Kristy, for the stunning photos.

To Esme and Richard, for the incredible ability to design stunning paper and willingness to join in on this venture.

To Tom, for his invaluable loan of photography equipment.

To Mum, Dad, Rach and Han, for your ongoing love, support and encouragement.

To Ben and Little E, for your unshakeable love and for being there amidst the occasional madness.

To Hugo and Florence, for resisting the urge to nibble anything of high value during the book's production.

To the Creator, my biggest supporter of all.

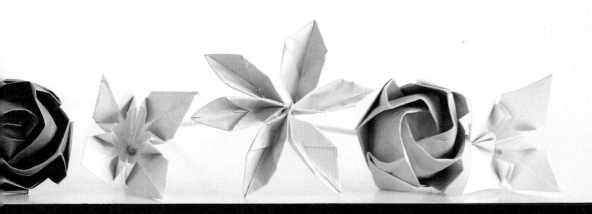

Publisher's thanks

We would like to thank Richard and Esme at Esme Winter for allowing us to use their beautiful paper designs throughout the book. Thank you to photographer Kristy Noble and designer Zoë Anspach for making this such a beautiful book. And thanks editor Cheryl Brown for her attention to detail and to Sophie Yamamoto for her assistance with the layout.

Picture credits

Step-by-step photography by Esther Thorpe. Main project photography by Kristy Noble. Cover photography by Rachel Whiting.

Background images provided by Esme Winter as follows: p5 & p140–141, JAZZ; p12–13 FREQUENCY; p56–57 & p144 ESKER; p112–113 PEGGY; back cover TWIST.

First published in the United Kingdom in 2016 by
Pavilion
1 Gower Street
London
WC1E 6HD

ISBN 978-1-91090-432-9

A CIP catalogue record for this book is available from the British Library.

10 9 8 7 6 5 4 3 2 1

Reproduction by Mission, Hong Kong
Printed and bound by 1010 Printing International Ltd, China

This book can be ordered direct from the publisher at www.pavilionbooks.com

PAVILION

Whatever the craft, we have the book for you – just head straight to Pavilion's crafty headquarters.

Pavilioncraft.co.uk is the one-stop destination for all our fabulous craft books. Sign up for our regular newsletters and follow us on social media to receive updates on new books, competitions and interviews with our bestselling authors.

We look forward to meeting you!

www.pavilioncraft.co.uk